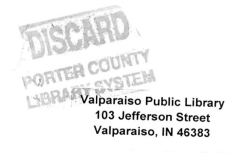

Operation
Code

Coding in the Science Lab

Scratch
3.0

By Kristin Fontichiaro and Colleen van Lent

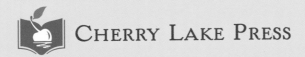

Published in the United States of America by Cherry Lake Publishing
Ann Arbor, Michigan
www.cherrylakepublishing.com

Series Adviser: Kristin Fontichiaro
Reading Adviser: Marla Conn, MS, Ed., Literacy specialist, Read-Ability, Inc.

Image Credits: ©DataBase Center for Life Science (DBCLS)/Wikimedia/Creative Commons Attribution 4.0 International/Changes were made by Cherry Lake Publishing, 4; ©OpenClipart-Vectors/Pixabay, 4, 20; ©UnboxScience/Pixabay, 4, 6, 12, 16, 20; ©DavidRockDesign/Pixabay, 4, 20; Various images throughout courtesy of Scratch; Sound effects obtained from https://www.zapsplat.com

Library of Congress Cataloging-in-Publication Data

Names: Fontichiaro, Kristin, author. | van Lent, Colleen, author.
Title: Coding in the science lab / by Kristin Fontichiaro and Colleen van Lent.
Description: Ann Arbor, Michigan : Cherry Lake Publishing, 2020. | Series: Operation code | Includes bibliographical references and index. | Audience: Grades 2-3.
Identifiers: LCCN 2019035735 (print) | LCCN 2019035736 (ebook) | ISBN 9781534159273 (hardcover) | ISBN 9781534161573 (paperback) | ISBN 9781534160422 (pdf) | ISBN 9781534162723 (ebook)
Subjects: LCSH: Scratch (Computer program language)–Juvenile literature. | Computer programming–Juvenile literature. | Science–Data processing–Juvenile literature.
Classification: LCC QA76.73.S345 F657 2020 (print) | LCC QA76.73.S345 (ebook) | DDC 005.13/3–dc23
LC record available at https://lccn.loc.gov/2019035735
LC ebook record available at https://lccn.loc.gov/2019035736

Cherry Lake Publishing would like to acknowledge the work of the Partnership for 21st Century Learning, a Network of Battelle for Kids. Please visit http://www.battelleforkids.org/networks/p21 for more information.

Printed in the United States of America
Corporate Graphics

NOTE TO READERS: Use this book to practice your Scratch 3 coding skills. If you have never used Scratch before, ask a parent, teacher, or librarian to help you set up an account at *https://scratch.mit.edu*. Read the tutorials on the website to learn how Scratch works. Then you will be ready for the activities in this book! You will practice using variables, if/then statements, copying code to other sprites, using effects to change a sprite's look, and more! Find all the starter and final programs at *https://scratch.mit.edu/users/CherryLakeCoding*.

Table of Contents

Robot in the Lab!

Rudy the Robot is loose in the science lab. Help Rudy make a big mess.

To copy our starter code, go to *https:// scratch.mit.edu/projects/319254293*.

This project has five **sprites**. The **lab bench** and group of **beakers** are **decorative** sprites. We will use **layers** to keep the sprites in the right order.

Pro Tip!
Scratch lets you see other people's projects. You can even copy the code to make them your own. Our code contains the sprites and sounds we will use in this book.

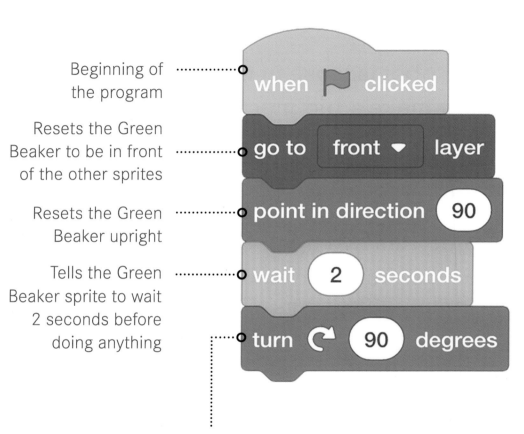

Beginning of the program ·········o **when** ⚑ **clicked**

Resets the Green Beaker to be in front of the other sprites ·········o **go to** front ▼ **layer**

Resets the Green Beaker upright ·········o **point in direction** 90

Tells the Green Beaker sprite to wait 2 seconds before doing anything ·········o **wait** 2 **seconds**

·········o **turn** ↻ 90 **degrees**

Turns the Green Beaker right ("90 degrees" means "right" in Scratch)

Pouring the Beaker

Rudy wants to mix the liquid in the Green and Yellow Beaker sprites.

Click on the Green Beaker sprite. Add the code and test it. Did you see the Green Beaker turn?

Pro Tip!

After testing your program, you might need to **reset** your sprite. This means putting it back in the right position, pointing the right way, or making sure it is in the front (so no other sprite is blocking it). Layers tell Scratch which sprites to put in front or back.

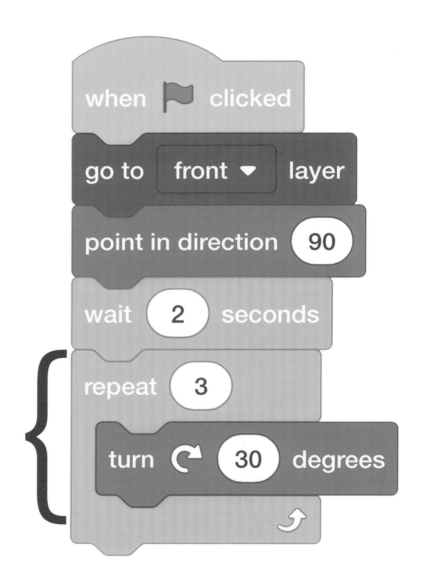

We replaced the *turn [90] degrees* **Motion** block with three 30-degree turns.

Slow Down That Beaker!

The Green Beaker moves, but it doesn't look like it is pouring. Let's make it turn by coding three small turns, 30 degrees for each. The Green Beaker will still turn 90 degrees because 30 + 30 + 30 = 90. This means the Green Beaker will end up in the same place, but the **animation** will look better.

Pro Tip!

When we use a *repeat* Control block, we're making a loop. Loops are sets of computer code that repeat. Loops are one way that coders can use fewer blocks and save time when building programs.

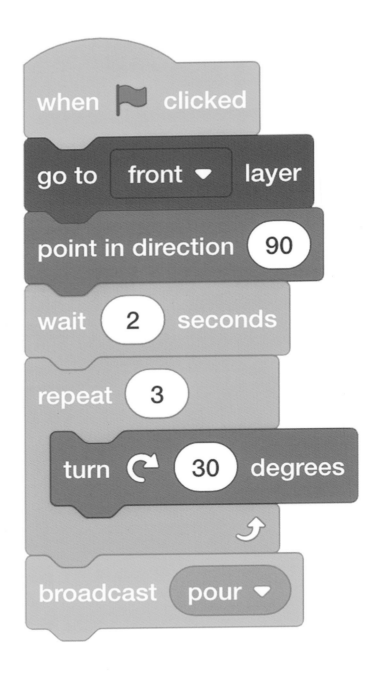

Sending a Signal

Let's change the color of the Yellow Beaker sprite when the Green Beaker sprite is poured into it.

One way is to have the Green Beaker sprite send out a special signal, called a broadcast. You can find the `broadcast  message1` block in the Events category.

Click "message 1." Choose "New message." Name it "pour."

Pro Tip!

Broadcasts don't appear to the viewer. They are invisible, or impossible to see. After a message is broadcast, it can be received by the other sprites.

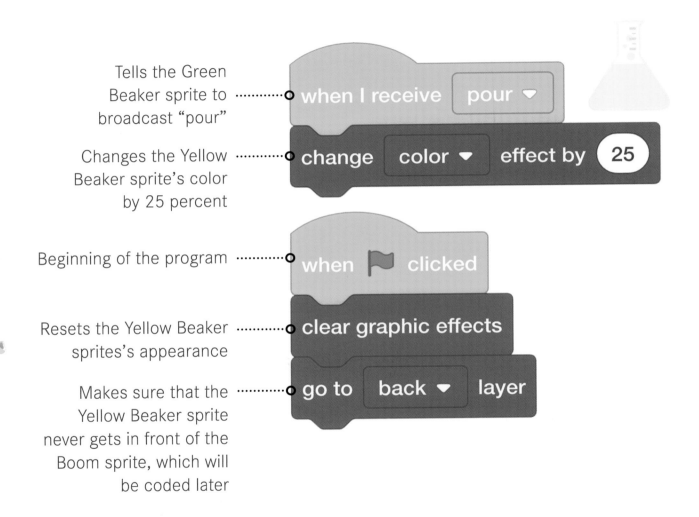

Tells the Green Beaker sprite to broadcast "pour" ·········○ when I receive pour ▼

Changes the Yellow Beaker sprite's color by 25 percent ·········○ change color ▼ effect by 25

Beginning of the program ·········○ when ⚑ clicked

Resets the Yellow Beaker sprites's appearance ·········○ clear graphic effects

Makes sure that the Yellow Beaker sprite never gets in front of the Boom sprite, which will be coded later ·········○ go to back ▼ layer

Changing the Yellow Beaker

Now click on the Yellow Beaker sprite. Let's code what it should do when it receives the "pour" broadcast from the Green Beaker sprite.

We want it to change colors so it looks like the liquids are mixing together. Click on the Yellow Beaker sprite and add the blocks shown. Read what is happening in the code.

Test your code at least twice.

Pro Tip!

Test what happens if you don't use the *clear graphic effects* **Looks** block in the beginning code. After running the code a few times, you'll notice that the beaker is never yellow again! This is one reason why we test our code more than once.

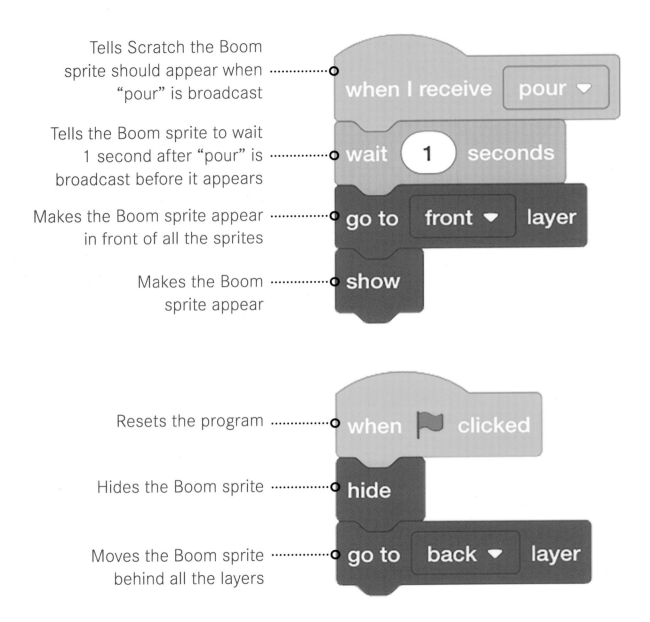

Tells Scratch the Boom sprite should appear when "pour" is broadcast ⋯⋯ **when I receive pour ▾**

Tells the Boom sprite to wait 1 second after "pour" is broadcast before it appears ⋯⋯ **wait 1 seconds**

Makes the Boom sprite appear in front of all the sprites ⋯⋯ **go to front ▾ layer**

Makes the Boom sprite appear ⋯⋯ **show**

Resets the program ⋯⋯ **when 🏴 clicked**

Hides the Boom sprite ⋯⋯ **hide**

Moves the Boom sprite behind all the layers ⋯⋯ **go to back ▾ layer**

BOOM!

Uh-oh! Something is about to explode.

Click on the Boom sprite. Similar to the Yellow Beaker sprite, we need two sets of code. One makes the Boom sprite appear after it receives the "pour" broadcast. The other resets the sprite's appearance at the start of the program.

Test your code at least twice.

Pro Tip!

Have you noticed that the lab bench is a sprite and not a backdrop? If it were a backdrop, then the robot could not appear behind it.

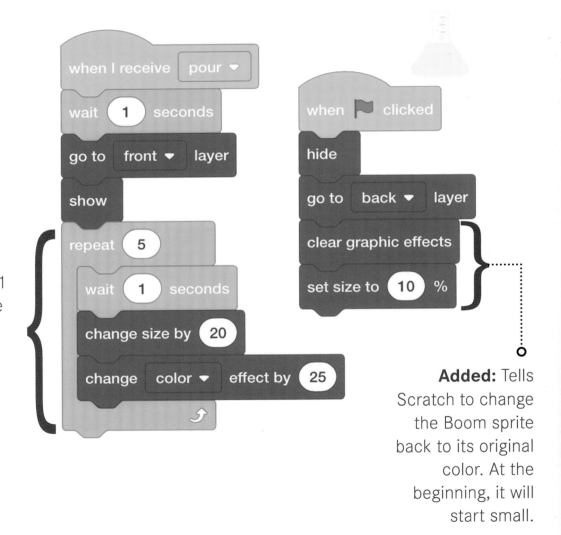

Added: Tells the Boom sprite to wait 1 second before getting bigger and changing colors. This pattern will repeat five times.

when I receive pour ▼

wait 1 seconds

go to front ▼ layer

show

repeat 5

wait 1 seconds

change size by 20

change color ▼ effect by 25

when ⚑ clicked

hide

go to back ▼ layer

clear graphic effects

set size to 10 %

Added: Tells Scratch to change the Boom sprite back to its original color. At the beginning, it will start small.

Making the Explosion Grow

The code works ... but the **explosion** doesn't have much pizzazz. What if the Boom sprite started small, then it got bigger and changed colors?

Click on the Boom sprite and add the code shown here. This will give you more practice with the *repeat, wait,* and *change color effect* blocks. Then test your code at least twice.

Pro Tip!

"Color" is just one way to use the *change effect* **Looks** block. You can also try "fisheye," "whirl," "pixelate," "ghost," and more!

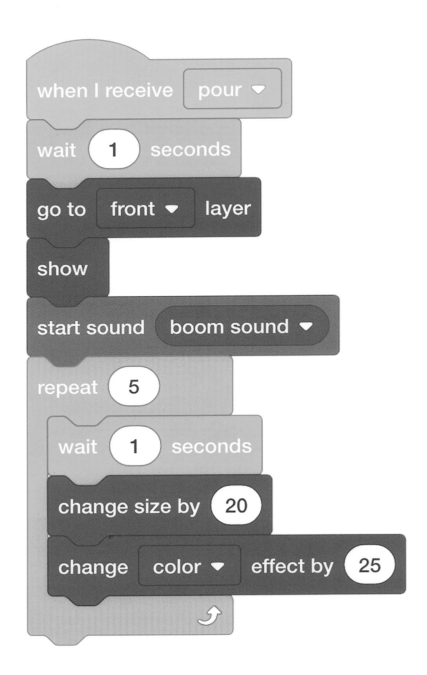

Adding Sound

What's an explosion without sound? Let's add some!

We **uploaded** a **custom** sound called "boom sound." In your Boom sprite code, add `start sound boom sound ▾`. You can find this block in the Sounds category.

Code this block in different places. What happens if you put it inside the *repeat* Control block?

Pro Tip!

Ask an adult to help you explore Scratch's many sound tools at *https://en.scratch-wiki.info/wiki/Sound*. You can record your own sound, edit how much sound you use, use Scratch's sounds, and more.

Keep Going!

You and Rudy made a real mess! He hopes you'll add even more **chaos**.

Here are some ideas:
- Code Rudy to say something.
- Ask an adult to help you record and upload a pouring sound for the Green Beaker sprite.
- Create your own sprite. Change its costume when the explosion happens.

What other ideas do you have?

Pro Tip!

To view our final code, please visit *https://scratch.mit.edu/projects/319244011*.

Glossary

animation (an-uh-MAY-shuhn) a way of using a series of pictures to create the appearance of movement

beakers (BEE-kurz) special glass containers used in science labs

chaos (KAY-ahs) complete and usually noisy disorder

custom (KUHS-tuhm) unique or one-of-a-kind

decorative (DEK-ur-uh-tiv) something that is just to look at

explosion (ik-SPLOH-zhuhn) when something blows up or splits apart into many pieces

lab bench (LAB BENCH) worktable in a science lab

layers (LAY-urz) ways of talking about which sprites are on top of each other

reset (ree-SET) to put things back the way they were at the beginning

sprites (SPRYTS) characters or objects in Scratch

uploaded (UHP-lohd-id) copied a file from your computer to Scratch, the Web, or another software

Find Out More

Books

LEAD Project. *Super Scratch Programming Adventure!*
San Francisco, California: No Starch Press, 2019.

Lovett, Amber. *Coding with Blockly.* Ann Arbor, Michigan:
Cherry Lake Publishing, 2017.

Websites

Scratch
http://scratch.mit.edu
Build your Scratch code online at this site.

Scratch Wiki
https://en.scratch-wiki.info
If you get stuck, ask an adult to help you look on this site for advice.

Index

About the Authors

Kristin Fontichiaro teaches at the University of Michigan School of Information. She likes working with kids on creative projects from coding to sewing to junk box inventions. She has written or edited almost 100 books for kids.

Colleen van Lent teaches coding and Web design at the University of Michigan School of Information. She has three cool kids and a dog named Bacon. She wishes she could touch her toes.